Play Together,
Stay Together

Play Together, Stay Together:

Games to Fortify Your Family

Brittany Thompson

CFI
Springville, Utah

ISBN 13: 978-1-59955-222-4

Published by CFI, an imprint of Cedar Fort, Inc., 2373 W. 700 S., Springville, UT 84663
Distributed by Cedar Fort, Inc., www.cedarfort.com

LIBRARY OF CONGRESS CATALOGING-IN-PUBLICATION DATA

Thompson, Brittany, 1986-
  Play together, stay together : games to fortify your family / Brittany Thompson.
    p. cm.
  Includes bibliographical references.
  ISBN 978-1-59955-222-4
  1. Family recreation. 2. Games. I. Title.

  GV182.8.T52 2008
  790.1'91--dc22

2008034997

Cover design by Angela Olsen
Cover design © 2008 by Lyle Mortimer
Edited and typeset by Melissa J. Caldwell

Printed in the United States of America

10 9 8 7 6 5 4 3 2 1

Printed on acid-free paper

Dedication

To my mom,
who taught me how to play

Contents

● ● ● ● ● ● ● ● ● ● ● ● ● ●

The family is the building block of society. It is a nursery, a school, a hospital, a leisure center, a place of refuge, and a place of rest. It encompasses the whole of society. It fashions our beliefs; it is the preparation for the rest of our lives.
—Margaret Thatcher, Former Prime Minister of Great Britain

A little bit of craziness once in a while perpetuates sanity.
—Gary Palmer, Professor, Brigham Young University

● ● ● ● ● ● ● ● ● ● ● ● ● ●

Acknowledgments

I feel so blessed to share my love of family recreation with you. This book truly has the power to change your house into a home where children feel loved, accepted, and safe from the troubles of the world. I hope you will use this book to transform your family into one full of trust and love.

First, I would like to thank my parents for filling me with a love for life and helping me to see the importance of having fun! I would also like to thank my wonderful husband for trying out so many games with me and for his constant love and support.

I gratefully acknowledge Cedar Fort for this wonderful opportunity to spread the message about families. I would especially like to thank Jeffrey Marsh for his guidance and direction in helping me to achieve my aspirations and providing me numerous opportunities for learning and growth. Thank you to my many editors, including Melissa, my parents, and my husband. Lastly, I would like to thank my Heavenly Father for providing me with so many opportunities to have joy in my life!

How a Game Is Made!

I am sure that games have been played since the beginning of time, and I hope they will keep being played forever. Most games start out very simple, and people add on rules the more they play, to make the game more complex. Being a professional at fun and games, I discovered some of the games in this book in classes, conferences, and group activities I have participated in. Friends have passed on other games to me, and others were acquired through study and research. I was especially privileged to be taught many of the games in this book from one of the best game players in the world: my mom. Because of the nature of creating and passing down games, citing exactly who first came up with a game is an extremely difficult task. In this book I have done this to the best of my ability and hope that readers will continue to pass these games on to their friends and family.

• • • • • • • • • • • • • • •

Chapter 1

Why Family Recreation?

• • • • • • • • • • • • • • •

"THE FAMILY THAT PLAYS TOGETHER, STAYS TOGETHER" should be a well-known phrase in the households of families everywhere. Many sources in the world today steal our time away from our families. Kids have a never-ending list of television shows and activities. The lives of our teenagers are consumed by homework and peers, while work, cleaning, and shopping seem to overwhelm parents. Although many of these tasks are important, family should always be at the top of our list! "The greatest work you will ever do, will be within the walls of your own home."[1]

It may seem like your children don't listen or learn from you, but believe me, they hear you. I recall a young mother whose two-year-old ran out into the street. Taking him by the arm, she scolded him firmly and told him, "Never, never do that again!" The next day in the grocery store, his dad told him not to touch something and that hurt the little boy's feelings. Holding onto his daddy's arm, he firmly told his dad to "Never, never do that again!" Even though not in a lesson form, this little boy knew his mom had been serious and thought if he needed to be serious about something, he should scold the same way. Surely, our children are always listening and learning from everything that goes on around them.

Lessons and love taught in the family have a great influence in the lives of children. So much power can be gained from strong family ties that each of us has the power to possess. A supportive family help raise a child's confidence. It gives them a place to turn when they need help and a refuge from the storms of life. Growing up, I always knew that I could come home and be loved, no matter what I faced in the world outside my home.

We need stronger families in our society. We need children to grow up knowing they are loved and that someone has faith in them—faith that they can accomplish anything! But sometimes kids won't sit and listen to a lesson. They already have enough school. We need to find a way to teach our children and strengthen family ties, while still promoting a fun-loving atmosphere. "How?" you ask. Well, that's exactly what this book is about.

What Do the Researchers Say?

Family leisure and recreation are crucial parts of establishing healthy relationships and successful communication within the family. It has been found that "in modern society, leisure is the single most important force developing cohesive, healthy relationships between husbands and wives and between parents and their children."[2] Leisure has the ability to let families step out of the box and look at their interactions through different eyes. It also allows families to work on how they function through an enjoyable process that allows them to see what they need to work on in a non-confrontational way. Because of this, leisure establishes the perfect environment for learning.

Family leisure gives us an opportunity to focus on things bigger than ourselves. By doing so, we have the ability to create certain character strengths in our family members such as kindness, self-control, gratitude, hope, and optimism. Recreation also gives family members the ability to model and practice these virtues, which they should be striving to develop throughout their lives.[3]

According to Aristotle, happiness is not a state of self-gratification where we only think about our own pleasure. Happiness comes from living and acting well as we focus on others. Those activities that take the spotlight off of self, and at the same time promote personal expressiveness, characterize leisure that leads to true happiness.[4]

Leisure in the family is one of the best ways to create activities leading to true happiness. It puts the spotlight on the group as a whole and not on one individual person. The supportive environment found in family leisure gives participants a chance to be themselves and supports their ability to express their feelings. This setting provides opportunities to promote family members' beliefs in themselves and each other.

Breaking the Age Barrier

Age barriers exist in every family, and many times make family relations difficult. Children do not know what it is like to be an adult and, more often than not, adults do not fully remember how it was to be a child. Siblings of various ages have differing attitudes and face different difficulties in their lives. Recreation helps to break the age barrier and put everyone on the same level. Many games have the opportunity to put members of the family in different roles, helping them to see life from the view of another family member. Recreation also has the ability to help our families appreciate and support one another in their differences. For these reasons, family recreation is the perfect solution to help build stronger family relationships.

So What?

This book is filled with different games and recreational activities that are great for families of all ages. The trick is in the application. Everybody can play a game with their family, and every game has benefits; yet, you may have learned that some games have greater benefits than others. Some allow you to learn something about each other and become closer as a family unit. I am here to tell you that this kind of situation can come from any game; it all depends on how you play.

Let's take a game that everyone knows: Capture the Flag! (If you are not in the category of "everyone," I apologize and direct you to page 35.) First, play the game without a plan. Let everyone run around, all trying to go for the flag. Whether you win or not, you know this could be done better. Then come together as a family and think of ways that you can capture the flag or ways to do it more quickly. Ask your family, "What are some strategies we could use to help us capture the flag?"

Using the skills of the different players would be one idea. Let the fast ones go after the flag and have others stand as distractions. Maybe you could map out different routes to the flag and have everyone try a different one. The possibilities are endless! Your family will see that everything goes smoother when everyone works together. After the game, talk to your family about what they have learned. How can this game help you to figure out how to solve problems in your family?

For example, say you are a little short on money, and you all need to help save. What have you learned from Capture the Flag that could help? Well, you could utilize the skills of your different family members and make a game plan. Perhaps you could save on utilities by turning off the lights when you leave a room or taking shorter showers. Some family members could be in charge of running around the house before everyone leaves, making sure all the lights are turned off. Others could help the family remember to take quicker showers by knocking on the door after five minutes, so they know to hurry up.

You see, if families learn to work together while they are having fun, it will be easy to carry the lessons over to more serious matters.

Now you may think, how will I know what questions to ask? Or how will I be able to make connections without my teens scoffing and my little kids getting lost? I, unfortunately, don't have a foolproof answer, but I do know that practice makes perfect. One key is to let your kids come up with the answers. Help them to feel confident and in control of the situation by coming up with possible solutions. The more your kids are a part of decisions, the more happy and cohesive your family will be.

Throughout this book, I will give you lots of ideas of games to play to help build family relationships. In the "So What?" application after each game, I will give you an idea of how each game can apply to your family. Keep in mind, however, that my suggestion is definitely not the only lesson that can be learned. Pay attention to your family. Don't be afraid to stop the game and chat about something. Any moment can be a learning moment. You can do it!

By engaging in recreational games and activities with your family, you will find amazing, positive changes in your family. Family members will start to have closer relationships with each other. Children will feel more connected as a family and achieve a clearer sense of identity. Family members will also have the opportunity to help each other develop stronger individual and familial values. Family recreation is essential in building successful, happy families.

NOTES

1. J. E. McCullock, *Home: The Savior of Civilization* [1924], 42, quoted in Conference Report, April 1935, 116.
2. R. B. Zabriskie and B. P. McCormick, "The Influence of Family Leisure Patterns on Perceptions of Family Functioning," *Family Relations: Interdisciplinary Journal of Applied Family Studies* 50, no. 3 (2004): 281.
3. M. A. Widmer, "Strengthening Marriage and Families Through Wholesome Recreation," *Marriage and Families* (Brigham Young University) (Summer 2004): 24–28.
4. G. D. Ellis and M. A. Widmer, "The Aristotelian Good Life Model: Integration of Values into Therapeutic Recreation Service Delivery," *Therapeutic Recreation Journal* 4 (1998): 290–302.

● ● ● ● ● ● ● ● ● ● ● ● ● ●

Chapter 2

Personal Space: Who Needs It?
Breaking Down Barriers in Your Family

● ● ● ● ● ● ● ● ● ● ● ● ● ●

Nose to Nose

Items Needed: Masking tape

Directions: Have every family member take a piece of masking tape, roll it into a ball, and stick the ball on their nose. Then, have everyone pair up and "smush" their noses together. Whoever pulls away with the other person's tape stuck to his nose goes on to the next round. The winner then finds another winner to see if he can pull off that tape too. Whoever ends up with everyone's tape, wins.

So What? Personal space can sometimes turn into a barrier that keeps your family apart. When kids are worried about others coming into their room or "space," it often creates tension in the family. This game can help loosen those barriers and help everyone have fun together while realizing that what's mine is yours . . . even our noses!

Yarn & Spoon Weave

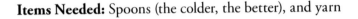

Items Needed: Spoons (the colder, the better), and yarn

Directions: Tie the spoon to a piece of very long yarn. Have everyone get in a line, with the first person holding the spoon. When the timer starts, the first person puts the spoon down her shirt and out the bottom of her pants. The next person has to then put the spoon up his pants and up his shirt. He then hands it off to the next person. The yarn and spoon go up and down until the last person has woven it through his clothes. Stop the timer and see how you did. Strategize to see if you can beat your record!

So What? Working together to get the best time helps the family learn to work together for a specific goal. When family members encourage each other, they always get things done faster and have a better time doing it.

Variations: After the yarn and spoon have gone through everyone, start the clock again and see how long it takes to get it out of everyone's clothes. This is also fun when two teams race against each other.

Clothespin Spin

Items Needed: Clothespins, and a timer

Directions: This game is hilarious and fun for the whole family. Give everyone five clothespins and set the timer for two minutes. The point of the game is to end up with the least amount of clothespins. The rules are:

1. You can only put one clothespin on a person at a time. You have to pin one on another person before going back to the first person.

2. If a clothespin is pinned on you, you can only get rid of it by pinning it on another person.

3. If you drop a clothespin while trying to pin it on someone, you are the one who has to pick it up.

Make boundaries. Then chase after your family members to pin your clothespins on them! Remember: If a clothespin is on you, you can only get rid of it by pinning it to another person. At the end of two minutes, see who has the least amount of clothespins stuck to them.

So What? Family members all have different strengths that help each other succeed in their lives. It is important and okay to be different because that is what makes families work. Some members are smaller, but just like in this game, that gives them an advantage in some ways. One person might be faster or more flexible than another and that also gives others' different advantages.

Family members need to look at other's strengths and not be jealous. They need to recognize what the different strengths are in each family member. When they do this, family members will never feel like someone is better than them, and they will know that each has a special role to play in their family.

Link Tag

● ● ● ● ● ● ● ● ●

Items Needed: Large playing area

Directions: Have everyone start off in groups of two and spread out around a large area. Each pair links their arms together. Pick one couple to be first, and choose one of them to be "it" and the other to be the runner. The person who is "it" has to try and tag the runner before he links arms with another team.

Once the runner links arms with another couple, the teammate hooked on the opposite side now has to run from the person who is "it." He tries to hook on to another team without getting tagged. The teammate cannot link back onto the same team he just came from. Once the "it" person tags another player on the run, the roles are switched. The runner is now "it" and the previous "it" person becomes the new runner.

So What? Family members are always there to save each other. A person may not actually be chasing them, but sometimes people might be mean or make fun of family members. In your family, stick together. Remember, you can "hook" on to each other for help, whenever you need it.

● ● ● ● ● ● ● ● ● ● ● ● ●

Hugger-pop

Items Needed: Balloons already blown-up, and a whole lot of love!

Directions: Have each person take one balloon for each member of the family (but not for themselves). Have everyone write the name of each family member on a different balloon. Then, help everyone to find a spot to put the balloons. When you say "go," everyone grabs a balloon, finds the family member whose name is written on it, and pops it with that family member. The trick is you can only pop the balloons by putting them between your stomachs and hugging each other tight. When the balloon is popped, run back, grab another balloon, and pop away! See how fast everyone can get all of the balloons popped.

So What? Sometimes, family members need a little reminder that they are loved. Physically hugging is a great way to help everyone feel loved and included in the family. Some kids might not want to stand in a circle and hug, but if you hug them while playing this game, they will be having so much fun, they won't even realize they are building family relationships! As children start to feel loved from all of their family members, home will truly become a sanctuary from the outside world and a wonderful place to be.

Variations: If your family is big enough, make this a race. Have two teams on one side of the room, with a pile of balloons for each team member on the other side. Have the teams race as partners to the end of the room, pop the balloon with a hug, and run back to tag the next set of partners.

Cracker Snapper

Items Needed: Newspapers, dental floss, and saltine crackers

Directions: Have everyone wear pants with belt loops on them. Each family member needs to take a saltine cracker and tie it to his back belt loop with a piece of floss. Next, everyone rolls up some newspaper. When you say go, everyone runs around, hitting the crackers with the rolled up newspaper. The person who still has a cracker at the end, wins!

So What? This game is perfect for just breaking down tension and having fun with your family. Families all have those days when they feel like if one more bad thing happens, they will explode. This is a perfect game to help everyone forget their troubles and have a good laugh.

Variations: To add another element of difficulty, have everyone hop around on one leg. If you have children of different ages, give each of them a different difficulty, based on their skill level, to make things more equal.

Kiss the Pig

Items Needed: An imagination!

Directions: In this game, the element of surprise is the key. Start out with everyone sitting in a circle. Cup both of your hands together and tell everyone that you have an imaginary pig in your hands. Then say, "I am going to kiss the pig on the . . ." and then you fill in the blank. For example, you could say, "I am going to kiss the pig on the right foot." Next, kiss the "imaginary" pig on the right foot, and pass the pig to the next person. Have her say the same phrase but with a different body part to kiss. When the "pig" gets around the whole circle, reveal that wherever they were going to kiss the pig, they now have to kiss the person on their left in that same spot.

So What? This is a hilarious game that gets everyone really laughing together. It also teaches that sometimes things in life will surprise us, but if we can laugh about them, we will never get "stuck in the mud."

Sardines

Items Needed: A family ready for fun!

Directions: This game is the opposite of hide and seek. One person goes and hides while everyone else counts. When you are done counting, everyone separates and starts to look for the one person hiding. When family members have found the person hiding, they hide together until everyone is squished in the hiding place. The first person to find the hiding spot gets to hide next. Sometimes this game gets tricky because there may not be a ton of room for everyone. The fun part is making sure that everyone fits!

So What? No matter what, we can always make room for everyone in our family. As a family, it is important to help everyone feel loved and included. Even if you feel like someone is taking up too much of your time or space, that person is a part of the family too. We need to make sure that everyone works together to fit all of our family members into our lives.

The Human Table

Items Needed: Two chairs, and one low stool

Directions: All right, this game gets a little tricky, but it is fun and teaches a great lesson. You will need to start out with two chairs and a stool that are all about the same height. Set the chairs and stool up to form a small square with one open corner.

Have the first person lie on one of the chairs with his back on the seat and his feet on the ground. Next, have the second person lie with his back on the thighs of the person and feet on the ground, using the second chair for support. Next, the third person will lie on the second person's thighs, using the stool for support. Finally, the fourth person will lie on the third person's thighs. The four people should be connected.

Everyone's back should be on top of another person's legs. When everyone is secure and leaning on the others' legs, pull the chairs out. You have made a human table![1]

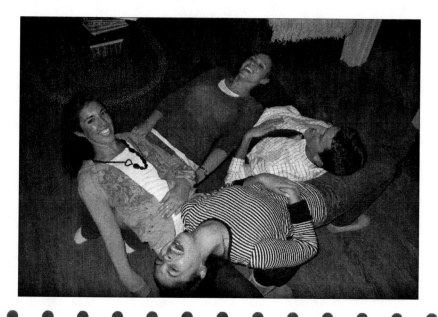

The Human Table

So What? Family members all have different capabilities, and they rely on each other for different things. While a younger sister may need help tying her shoes, the older brother that ties her shoes may need help from a parent with homework. The fact is, family members can't make it alone, and that's why they have each other. Each person in your family is important. All family members need to support each other in order to be the best they can. A table without a leg is just a piece of wood!

Variations: If you want to make this game extra tricky, try getting a glass of water and setting it on the "table." See just what kind of balance your family has!

NOTE

1. The Van Overbeek Family.

Chapter 3

Playing with Your Food:
Learning to Work Together as a Family

Tortilla Toss

Items Needed: Tortillas, and a wide brimmed hat (like one you would wear at a Mexican fiesta!)

Directions: Have one person put on the hat and stand back from the rest of the group. Give everyone a chance to see how many tortillas they can throw into the hat while the person is moving around. (Probably not very many.) Then, have everyone pick up their tortillas and try tossing them into the hat again while the person with the hat is standing still. Last, have the person with the hat move, trying to catch the tortillas in the hat. Each time see who can get the most tortillas into the hat.

So What? Cooperation is very important when family members want to get things done in their family. Families need to make sure that they are always working together and helping each other to accomplish their goals. When family members are going against each other or fighting, it is hard to make any progress. But if they work together, they can do things they could not do alone.

Ice Cream Sculpting

Items Needed: A half gallon of ice cream for every team, and trash bags (to contain the mess!)

Directions: This activity will help the future architects in the family shine. You will need to break your family into teams, and give each team their own half gallon of ice cream. The easiest is the ice cream in the thin, square cardboard, so you can take off all the sides and just have the block of ice cream. (Luckily that's the cheapest kind too!) Make sure to put trash bags or some kind of cover over the table, or wherever you are doing the game, and let the teams go wild. See who can make the most creative sculpture with their ice cream. You had better give a time limit though, or you'll end up with nothing but soup!

So What? All of the kids in my family had pretty big imaginations, and if your family is like mine, we all would have our own ideas about what would be the best thing to sculpt.

During this activity, everyone has a chance to work together and incorporate all the ideas into the sculpture. This is a perfect time to help your children remember that everyone's ideas are important, and that they need to be respectful to others no matter how good they feel their idea is.

Leaning Tower of Cheesa

Items Needed: Easy cheese, and plates for each team

Directions: Have everyone get in partners and give each partnership a bottle of squeeze-cheese and a plate. Delegate one partner to be the squeezer and the other one to help hold up the tower. Say "go" and start building. See who can make the tallest tower out of their cheese. Only the designated partner can use his hands. Don't let it lean too far, or you might have a falling tower of cheesa!

So What? Family members need to make sure they have a good balance in their lives. When families try to cram too many things into their schedule at once, sometimes they end up falling apart. Family members need to make sure that they fit the most important things in their schedule, like family activities, and still retain their sanity. If they can't, something has got to go!

Pudding Painting

Items Needed: Large pieces of cardstock, and lots of pudding

Directions: Here's a chance for everyone to get messy! Give everyone a piece of cardstock, the bigger the better. Make up a big bowl of pudding, and let everyone dig in! Using only hands, everyone will create a picture with the pudding. It will be the best tasting art project ever!

So What? Being creative with your family helps everyone appreciate each other. It also gives everyone the opportunity to build up family members with compliments. This art project will bring lots of laughs. You might just end up a little closer than when you started.

● ● ● ● ● ● ● ● ● **Cherry Spit**

Items Needed: Cherries with pits

Directions: Bring a big bowl of cherries (with pits) to a place that can really get messy. Have everyone take a cherry and eat the outside of it, leaving the pit. Then have a contest to see who can spit the farthest. If you have a large piece of butcher paper, you can label everyone's pit so you know whose is whose.

So What? Sometimes in life, you will find little pits. You will think something is going to be great and then may be disappointed later. This game will help us learn to make the best out of those pits in our lives. If something's too hard to swallow, make some fun out of it!

● ● ● ● ● ● ● ● ● ● ● ● ●

Fruit Loop Toss

Items Needed: Peanut butter, fruit loops, and trash bags

Directions: Have everyone get into groups of two. Make sure the whole family is in clothes that can get dirty. (Trash bags to cover up clothes might be a good idea as well.)

Have one person from each team sit in a chair facing her teammate and cover her clothes up with the trash bag so they don't get too dirty. Next, give the player standing up some peanut butter and have her smear it all over the other person's face. When finished, have the clean partner take five steps back.

Then give each partner a bag of fruit loops. In thirty seconds, see how many fruit loops each team can get to stick to the peanut butter face. When you are all done . . . it's payback time! Switch places. Add up the total amount of fruit loops to decide on the winning team.

So What? If any of you (or your children) have ever watched *The Magic School Bus,* Miss Frizzle would always say we need to be willing to "Get messy!" and "Make mistakes!" These words are very true when it comes to our families.

Families need to create an atmosphere in their home where everyone feels like they can let their hair down and be themselves. This game can help your family let go and realize there is something special about family that you can't get anywhere else. They love you no matter what . . . even when you have peanut butter all over your face!

Graham Cracker Architecture

Items Needed: Lots of graham crackers, frosting, and small candies

Directions: For this one you can choose what kind of accessories you want to have (just make sure they are all edible). Give all members a set of crackers, and let them start creating something out of their supplies. Some little kids may need help, but try to get everyone to make something different. In the end, put the graham cracker creations all on display and have everyone tell about it. Then, give everyone a chance to say something nice about that person's project.

So What? Doing individual projects with the family has great value in helping everyone appreciate the creativity in one another. Positively commenting on the work of each family member will help the family to learn how to compliment and support each other. Support is crucial to building strong homes and families. This is a perfect way to teach your family how to give that support to others.

Dinner Is Served (Kind of)

Items Needed: Butcher paper, and crayons

Directions: Cover your table with butcher paper and let your kids create the tablecloth. Have them draw dinner, a scenic mountain view, and anything else they can create. Let their imaginations go wild. You then have some time to cook dinner without interruptions—I hope!

So What? This activity will teach your kids to work together and also help them to learn the right way to set the table.

Variations: Have your older kids draw where all of the silverware and plates go. Then have them help their younger siblings set the table by matching the real objects to the drawings.

Toothpick and Gumdrop Modern Art

Items Needed: Toothpicks, gumdrops, and blindfolds

Directions: Sit around a table and put all of the toothpicks and gumdrops in the middle so everyone can reach them. Tell everyone you are going to give them ten minutes to build the tallest tower of gumdrops while they are blindfolded. Once everyone puts on their blindfolds, say "go." After ten minutes say "stop," take the blindfolds off, and take a look at what they have done.

Next, have everyone choose a partner. They will still be blindfolded this time, but they will have a partner, and they will be able to make a plan before they start building. Give everyone a few minutes to make their plan, and then say "go." After ten minutes, compare the towers to see if the second tower is taller.

So What? Many kids just want to be left alone to do things themselves. They don't want anyone's help. Sometimes this could cause problems. This game helps family members realize that things work out better when they work together. When we take time to plan ahead with someone else, and we both help to accomplish it, we will get faster, taller, and better results!

Variations: If you don't have gumdrops, try using marshmallows or gummy bears. Anything sticky will do. The messier, the better!

Chapter 4

Everyone Plays:
Games for All Sizes, Ages, and Abilities

Kickball

Items Needed: A rubber ball and a baseball field (or other large area)

Directions: This game is played on a baseball field and has most of the same rules as baseball. The only difference is the ball. You will need a rubber ball or a soccer ball. Instead of throwing the ball and hitting it with a bat, roll the ball to the "batter" or kicker, who then kicks it as far as he can. The kicker runs to as many bases as he can, but he better stay on a base before he gets tagged with the ball. The team with the most runs at the end of the game wins.

So What? Everyone can play and have fun in this game! Everyone's different talents will help out in some way. Bigger is not necessarily better, so the baby of the family might just be the MVP!

Volleyball Battleship

Items Needed: A volleyball, a volleyball net or a rope, and sheets

Directions: If you don't have a volleyball net for this game, you can tie a rope between two trees. Hang sheets or blankets over the net or rope so you can't see through to the other side. Split your family into two teams. Have the teams choose a side and lie anywhere on the floor on their side of the net.

Once everyone has chosen a spot on the floor, they cannot move from it. With a soft volleyball (so if someone is hit, they won't be hurt), have each member take a turn throwing the ball over the net. If someone is hit, they are sunk. The team who sinks all of the other team's ships first, wins.

So What? This is a great game for the whole family to play. Everyone can take part and have fun while working together with a team. Providing experiences for your family to laugh and have fun together will help bring unity. This game helps everyone feel excited to come together again!

● ● ● ● ● ● ● ● **Broom Hockey**

Items Needed: Brooms for everyone in the family, and a ball

Directions: Break into teams and make sure each person has a broom. You can play on a hard surface or a grassy field. A soccer ball is the most effective "puck." Set up two goals or goal lines, and say "go!" Using only brooms, work with your teammates to push the ball through the goal.

So What? Learning to work as a team is crucial for families, and teamwork learned through playing games generalizes to many different aspects of family life. As you make plans with family members and execute them together, you learn how to fix problems and disagreements by working as a team.

Variations: If the skill level of the members in your family varies greatly, try giving them different-sized brooms or maybe even a dustpan. Making sure everyone has a bit of a challenge keeps the game engaging and helps everyone have a good time.

● ● ● ● ● ● ● ● ● ● ● ● ●

Funnel Catch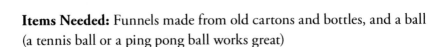

Items Needed: Funnels made from old cartons and bottles, and a ball (a tennis ball or a ping pong ball works great)

Directions: Cut a bleach bottle or a gallon milk carton in half to make the perfect glove for this game. Make sure everyone has some kind of funnel to catch with, and start throwing the ball around. After your family starts getting the hang of it, make goals of how many times you can pass it to each other without anyone dropping it. Back up a few feet and see how far away you can get without dropping the ball. Your family will have a blast with this fun spin on playing catch![1]

So What? Sometimes we put family members into categories like "athletic" and "clumsy." These categories can really stick and affect a family member much longer than we realize. In order to keep this from happening, put a little twist on a sport that everyone is used to playing. In doing so, you will keep a level playing field in your family. Also, when competing together, like you do when you make goals in this game, you will be able to practice and excel as a family—not just as individuals.

NOTE

1. A. Heaton, *Double Fun* (Springville, UT: Cedar Fort, Inc., 1999), 3.

● ● ● ● ● ● ● ● **Magazine Hunt**

Items Needed: Lots of old magazines

Directions: Scrounge up as many old magazines as you can. Split your family into two teams with an even amount of magazines for each team. Give both teams a list of at least twenty items they need to find in the magazines. This list could include toothpaste, a camera, someone smiling, a boat, the word "family", a food mom likes to eat, and so forth. The list can consist of anything from photos of different items to names or letters. Set the timer and see which team can find the most items in ten minutes.

So What? Almost anyone can recognize pictures or words, and that's what makes this game fun for the whole family! Everyone is able to play and contribute to the game. Families who have a wide range of ages will find this relevant. Everyone wants to be an important part of the family.

● ● ● ● ● ● ● ● ● ● ● ● ●

Water Balloon Volleyball

Items Needed: Water balloons, two sheets, and a volleyball net or a rope

Directions: With a volleyball net in the middle of a large space (or a rope tied between two trees), split your family into two teams and put a team on each side of the net. Give each team a sheet and have them spread out around it. Put a filled water balloon in the middle of one team's sheet. Everyone must work together to bring the sheet down and then up, in order to fling the "ball" toward the other team. They catch it on the other side, and do the same thing back. See how many times you can catch it back and forth. Try to beat your record!

So What? To make this work, everyone on the team must pull the sheet down and then launch it back up at the same time. If one person is lower than everyone else, the water balloon will not go in the direction you want it to. Just like the game, when family members have a goal that they want to accomplish, they need the whole family to work together. If one person is not supportive, it won't work. Families need everyone in order to have success!

Variations: If you are not interested in getting wet, this game will work great with a large rubber or beach ball.

Three-legged Soccer

Items Needed: Bandanas or pieces of material, and a soccer ball

Directions: Just like a three-legged race, have everyone get in partners, and use bandanas or a piece of material to tie one of their legs together with a leg of their partner. Practice walking and running while being attached to your partner. Set up goals and let the soccer game begin!

So What? This game is perfect in learning to work together as a family. Each group will have the opportunity to make up strategies and see what works for them. Next time you see family members fighting over who's turn it is to do the dishes, try using these strategies from the game. If they can't remember, tie their hands together, and try three-handed dish-doing. (Glass dishes are not recommended!)

Balloon Stomp

Items Needed: Balloons, and string

Directions: Have all family members blow up a balloon and tie it to their ankle with a piece of string. On the signal, everyone tries to stomp on the other balloons and pop them. The best way to avoid getting your balloon popped is to hop around on one foot. (That's also the funniest way to play the game!) Once your balloon is popped, go to the outside of the playing area and cheer on the rest of your family.

The person left with his balloon unpopped is the winner, but will probably not have a balloon for very long. Now it's everyone else's chance to go after that person, who probably popped most of the balloons.

So What? This fun game is perfect for the whole family. It doesn't matter what size you are; it all depends on how you use your size. Sometimes siblings may feel like they get the raw end of the deal because they are the smallest, the oldest, or just squished in the middle. In this game, family members can use their position and size to their advantage. Everyone's place in the family is different, but all are just as important and special as the next.

● ● ● ● ● ● ● ●   **Capture the Flag**

Items Needed: Two flags (any item really), and a large area

Directions: Split the family into two teams. Have the teams pick an item to be their flag. Get the two teams together to make up the boundaries and to show what their flag is. Split the boundaries in half. Let each team pick a spot that will be "jail" for the other team's members who are tagged. Give the teams some time to hide their flag.

At the start of the game, team members are on their own side. If you go onto the other team's side, you are on dangerous ground. If someone on that team tags you, you are in jail. The only way to get out of jail is for one of your team members to tag you without being caught.

The point of the game is to find out where the other team's flag is, capture it, and bring it to your side without getting caught. You may want to make rules for how far away each team must be from their flag and jail (no babysitting, for example). Also, if a teammate is tagged from jail, decide whether he gets to walk back to his team without anyone tagging them or if he needs to dodge the other team.

So What? Just like in this game, all families have goals they are working on, whether it's to help each other remember chores or to be kinder to each other. With planning, these goals can be accomplished much more successfully. The team who wins is usually the team with a better plan. Just like in the game, your family will run much smoother when you take the time to plan and work out your struggles and goals together.

● ● ● ● ● ● ● ● ● ● ● ● ●

Chapter 5

It's a Crack-Up!:
Building Relationships through Laughter

• • • • • • • • • • • • •

Zoom and Erk

Items Needed: Straight faces, and tight lips

Directions: This hilarious game of "tight lips" is perfect to loosen up any group. The trick in this game is that no one is allowed to show their teeth at any time. Have everyone get in a circle and choose one person to start. The first person says "zoom" to the person sitting to the right of them and to pass it on, that person says "zoom" to the person sitting to the right of them. If someone wants to change the direction, just turn to the person who said "zoom" to you and yell "erk."

Now the direction of play has changed and the players continue saying "zoom" to the person sitting to the left of them until someone else says "erk" and the direction is changed once again. Be creative in how you say "zoom" or "erk"—you are trying to get the person next to you to laugh and show their teeth. But beware! The crazier you say "zoom" to your neighbor, the crazier she says it to you. If you laugh, you had better keep your lips tight or you are out!

Zoom and Erk   ● ● ● ● ● ● ● ●

So What? This is the perfect game to lighten up the mood and just have fun together. Sometimes family members can get so caught up in their daily routine, that they forget to have fun. Laughing as a family is a perfect way to make your home a happy one!

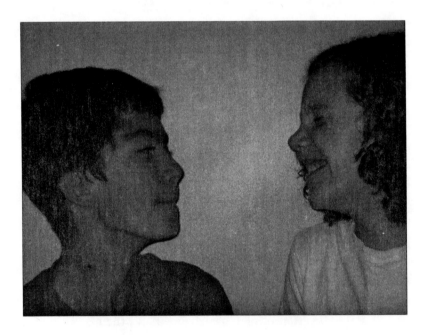

● ● ● ● ● ● ● ● ● ● ● ● ●

Crazy Creators

Items Needed: Random items around the house

Directions: Imagination is a crucial part of this game, which is perfect for a family of all ages. Gather up a few random objects from around the house such as an inner tube, a remote control, kitchen utensils, a basketball, a toothbrush, a football, and so forth. Split into two teams and pick one object to be used first. The first team has to come up with a funny use for the item that can't be its obvious use. For example, an inner tube may be used as a wheel on a car, a seat for someone who's just hurt their tailbone, a slip-and-slide for ants, or an opera hat for a large-headed woman. The next team then has to come up with another use for the item. The teams go back and forth until no more uses can be found. The team who comes up with the last use gets a point. Then, you move on to the next object. Before you know it, you'll be rolling on the floor with laughter.

So What? It is so important for families to learn to be creative. When family members are able to think out of the box, they will be better able to solve problems and have fun no matter where they are. Who thought that a spatula, an inner tube, and a remote control could be so much fun!

Shuffle Your Buns

Items Needed: Chairs for everyone

Directions: Chairs are placed in a circle, with enough chairs for everyone in the group. One person is chosen to be in the middle, which leaves an empty chair. This person has to try and sit in the empty chair while the people sitting down have to try and shuffle over in order to prevent them from sitting down. When the person in the middle is finally able get a seat, the person to the right is now in the middle and buns will be shuffling all over again![1]

So What? This is a hilarious game that your family will want to play over and over. Games like this that promote fun and laughter within your family will help each member to feel a bond with the others. Being able to laugh together creates a safe environment where children feel they can go for love and support.

NOTE

1. M. Yaconelli and W. Rice, *Super Ideas for Youth Groups* (Grand Rapids, MI: Zondervan Publishing House, 1979), 36.

● ● ● ● ● ● ● ● ● **Stick Pull**

Items Needed: A strong stick or piece of PVC pipe

Directions: All you need for this game is a stick. Have two family members sit on the floor across from each other with their feet touching. Both family members hold one stick right above their feet. On the signal, both family members pull as hard as they can until one of them pulls the other person over or pulls the stick out of their hands.

So What: Every family needs to withstand a little pull once in a while. Family members need to have a sense of humor and find the ability to laugh at themselves and at each other. This will help family members to not get their feelings hurt and to quickly forgive when someone says or does something that hurts their feelings.

Do You Love Your Neighbor?

Items Needed: Chairs for everyone but one person

Directions: Start this game in a big circle, where everyone has a chair except the person standing in the middle. The person in the middle asks someone, "Do you love your neighbor?" The person then answers either yes or no. If the person says, "Yes, I do love my neighbor," the two people sitting next to her have to switch seats. Meanwhile, the person in the middle tries to get into one of their seats.

If the person says no, she says who she does love. For example, "No, but I do love people who are wearing socks," or "No, but I do love anyone with brown eyes." Then, anyone with brown eyes or wearing socks has to stand up and run to switch seats. Be quick, you don't want to get stuck in the middle!

So What? "I love you" should not be a foreign phrase in our families. Using it in a game like this will help it to become more familiar. Family members all need to hear this phrase. Tell your family that you love them all of the time. Doing so will help your whole family feel safe and never question the love and acceptance they feel in your family.

Sock It to 'Em

Items Needed: Lots of feet with socks on them

Directions: Have everyone take off their shoes, leaving on their socks. Make sure you have a big enough space for everyone to run around and that everyone knows the boundaries. When you say "go," everyone needs to try and pull off the socks of the other players while still keeping theirs on. Once both socks are off, you are out. The person left with a sock on is the winner.[1]

So What? This is the perfect game to get everyone to loosen up and just have fun together. Sometimes family members forget to stop and have a little fun. This is a great way to remind your family that life is *fun* and that having fun with your family makes it even better!

NOTE

1. J. Byl, *Co-Ed Recreational Games* (Champaign, IL: Human Kinetics, 2002), 68.

Leg Wrestling

Items Needed: Just space to play

Directions: Here is a game of skill and agility that can have winners of many different shapes and sizes! Have two family members lie on the floor opposite each other. Each person's head should be next to the other person's thigh. Count to three. On each count have the family members lift up their inside legs. On three, their inside legs hook together. The person who makes the other do a backwards summersault is the winner.

So What? Family members love their family so much! They may put up a fight, but in the end, they'll do flips for each other.

Buzurk!

Items Needed: Paper, and space to run

Directions: Before the game starts, write down as many animals as you can think of, two of each kind (dog, dog, cat, cat, and so forth). Cut the paper up with a single animal on each piece. The point of this game is to find all of your matches without talking (animal noises are acceptable).

If you have a chicken, you need to act like a chicken until you find another family member acting like a chicken. When you have found your match, that animal is done and you go on to another one. If you have been acting like an animal for a while and you still can't find your match, please stop looking so silly and move to another animal. Split up the animals among the family members, and go for it. Remember there is no talking. The first person to find all of his matches is the winner.

So What? Family members need to learn to let loose around each other. They need to feel comfortable around each other so when they need help or someone to talk to, they know where they can go. This game is perfect for letting loose. How funky is your chicken?

Variations: If you have a larger group, put the papers in the middle with just enough pairs for the amount of people in the group. Have everyone sit in a circle around the papers and when you say go, have everyone run to the center, grab a paper, and start acting like the animal. When they find their partner, have them run back to the edge of the circle and sit down. The last couple to get back is out and takes their papers with them. Throw the rest of the paper in the middle, and keep playing until you have winners!

Whizzer Ball

Items Needed: An old nylon, and rags or socks

Directions: This game must be played outside with a lot of room for running. Take the leg of an old nylon and stuff the bottom with rags or socks. Take turns twirling the nylon around and letting it fly into the air. Then, have everyone try to catch the crazy whizzer before it hits the ground. The person who catches it gets to throw it next.[1]

So What? Games like this are perfect for laughing and getting your family out in the fresh air to have fun. Getting outside and playing helps everyone forget their worries. What better group is there to forget your worries with than your family?

NOTE

1. Parents Magazine Publisher, *Family Fun Book: Hobbies, Games, Party Ideas for Parents and their Children* (New York: The Parents' Institute, 1950), 43.

Might I Bite?

Items Needed: Paper, and tape

Directions: For this game, you need small pieces of paper with names of different animals on each one. Have each person in your family tape one of the pieces of paper on their head, without looking, so that everyone else can see. When you say go, everyone starts asking yes or no questions about the animal they are. "Might I bite?" "Do I have scales?" "Do I smell bad?" All players try to figure out what animal they are first. Time yourselves as a family, and try to beat the time it takes for everyone to figure it out.[1]

So What? This is a great game for learning and fun! Just like family members need to help each other in order to win the game, they also need to make sure to help each other every day in all that they do. When family members take the time to care and help each other out, they will find themselves with a much happier home!

Variations: Change what you put on the pieces of paper in order to make the game easier or harder. If one of your children is studying the presidents in school, write down names of presidents for your family to play with. Just think how much better studying will be with the whole family involved!

NOTE

1. "Games," Family Fun, www.Familyfun.com (accessed April 1, 2008).

Musical Hats

Items Needed: Enough hats for everyone but one person, and music

Directions: This is just like the well-known game musical chairs except you play with hats (and the strategy is much different). Have everyone sit in a circle with enough hats in the middle for everyone but one person. Let the music play for a while. When you stop it, let everyone dive for the hats. Everyone must put it on their head as fast as they can. Once they have it on their head they are safe, but if it is only in their hands, stealing is completely fair. The person left without a hat takes one of the hats and steps out. The rest of the group continues to play in like manner until there is one winner.

So What? This is a hilarious game that helps family members to learn to be a good sport. Many children fret if they lose a game or if something doesn't work out how they want it to. It is important to help every family member realize that winning isn't everything, and they can have fun no matter what, especially when you have children of different ages.

Variations: If you have many different ages in your family, give some of your family members challenges, like playing with their left hand or sitting backwards in the circle. By doing so, you will create a more even playing field.

Name Game

Items Needed: Paper, a bowl, and a timer

Directions: Start out by giving everyone ten small pieces of paper, and have them write the name of a different famous person (president, cartoon character, basketball player, and so forth) on each piece of paper. When you are all done, fold the papers in half and mix them all up in a hat. Split into two teams and choose one team to go first.

There are three rounds in this game. During the first round, the first team picks one person to go first. The family member comes up, and in thirty seconds, tries to have his team guess as many of the names as possible that he pulls out of the hat. When the first team is done, the second team gets a chance to pick a player and see how many names they can guess in thirty seconds. During this first round, the teams can say **anything they want** as long as it's not the name on the paper. They cannot use letters or any body movements, but they can do impressions, give clues, or whatever they need to get their team to guess the name. Keep track of how many names each team has correctly guessed. The teams continue alternating turns with different people until you run out of names. Round two then starts.

Put all the names back in the hat, mix them up, and play the game exactly how you did the first time, except you can now only say **one word** to describe each name. Since you have already heard all of the names, this won't be as hard as it seems—I promise!

When you get through all of the names for round two, put all the names back in the hat once more. Play round three the same way, except this time, you **cannot say anything**—nope, not a word. You can only use body movements, like in charades!

Name Game ● ● ● ● ● ● ● ● ●

So What? This game is fun for the whole family. I promise you'll have lots to laugh and tease about later. Making funny memories with your family is an important key to keeping families close together and helping each member enjoy the company of the others.

Guess Who?

Items Needed: A drawing board, and markers

Directions: You really get a chance to laugh with each other in this game. Get a big board you can draw on and something to write with. Write everyone's name on small pieces of paper, and put them in a bowl. Have one person at a time choose a name. Then, using your best artistic skills, draw that person in the family so that everyone else can "guess who"!

So What? Laughing at yourself is an important coping mechanism in life. No one is perfect, and learning to laugh will help family members to pick themselves up when they fall. So what if someone draws you with a huge nose—life is too short to take everything seriously.

Variations: Make this a race and see who can get someone to "guess who" the fastest. You can also split everyone into teams and have two people drawing at the same time. You may be surprised by what you look like in your five-year-old's eyes!

Crack-up

Items Needed: Plastic bowls, ribbons, and eggs

Directions: Divide into teams or partners. Take a bowl that you can put holes in, and loop a ribbon or a shoelace through a hole in each side of the bowl. Tie the bowl, open side up, to the top of someone's head. Have that person stand on one side of the yard. (Yes, I definitely recommend doing this game outside!) Have the second person stand on the other side with a dozen eggs. See how many of the eggs each team can catch in their bowl. Make sure that everyone gets a chance to be the one with the bowl on their head—especially Dad!

So What? When family members help each other, things might get a little messy. But hey, what are families for?

Variations: If you don't want to get quite as messy, do this with large marshmallows, or water balloons if it's hot.

Chapter 6

Picture-perfect Problem Solving

Group Charades

Items Needed: Paper, and large imaginations

Directions: Write the names of different items on small slips of paper (washing machine, the Eiffel Tower, kitchen table, and so forth). Split your family into two groups and have the first group pick out a slip of paper. Whatever is written on the paper, the group needs to act out as a team. No one person is allowed to act alone—each group member must have a part in the charade. Once the other team has guessed, trade off and see which group can be the most creative with all of their members.

So What? Working as a team and including everyone is an important family trait. Many times it would just be easier to do something alone, but it is sometimes important to include someone for different reasons and not just because it is easy. When the family can learn to include their other members in activities or work, relationships within the family will truly flourish.

Don't Lose Your Marbles

Items Needed: Marbles, and tubing (a paper towel or wrapping paper roll, or short pieces of PVC pipe)

Directions: If possible, cut some of your tubing down the sides to make an open tube, and leave other pieces fully enclosed. Everyone should have one piece of tubing and hold it to create some kind of a trough for the marble to roll down. The object of this game is to work together to pass the marble from one trough to the other and see how fast you can get the marble across the room without it falling on the ground. It may be tricky with the different heights and sizes of your family, but figure out how to use this to your advantage.

So What? To get this game to work, everyone needs to be willing to work together, be flexible, and be willing to listen to other people. If everyone tried to be the leader in this game, the marble would fall, and the family would never win! Just like how someone needs to take the lead in the game to make it work, families sometimes need to let one of the siblings or parents take the lead. It is okay to let others be in charge when they have a good idea! Family members need to learn to be good leaders *and* followers.

● ● ● ● ● ● ● ●   **Color Me Yours**

Items Needed: Paint, paint brushes, and paper

Directions: Pair up everyone in your family. Have each pair paint a beautiful picture. Now most likely, each person's idea of "beautiful" will be different. This could cause conflict in some cases, but encourage everyone to work together and make sure their picture is a collaboration of both people and not just one person's ideas. In the end, you may not have a perfect picture, but you may have a family that has learned a bit about working together.

So What? Always getting your way and doing the things you want to do is not conducive to a happy family. When families are working on something, they need to make sure to take everyone's ideas and work toward having everyone being happy with the final result. Family members may not agree with someone's idea, but sometimes it is important to let others do it their way (even if it may not be the best idea).

● ● ● ● ● ● ● ● ● ● ● ● ● ●

Electric Fence

Items Needed: Rope, and two trees close together

Directions: This game works the best outside. Between two trees, tie a rope about four feet off the ground. As a family, you now need to figure out how you are going to get everyone over the "fence" without touching it. (No going underneath!) Be careful to think about everyone you need to get across and don't let anyone drop![1]

So What? This is a perfect game to help your family work together and learn to solve problems as a group. To solve this problem, like many you will encounter, you need to look at the different abilities and skills of everyone in the family. It takes a total group effort for everyone to make it over the fence. If someone just hops over without discussing it with the group, they may be leaving one of the other family members stranded. "Family" includes many different people and solving problems will never work if the only one you are worried about is yourself.

Variations: This game can also be played by tying a hula hoop a few feet above the ground and having everyone get each other through with out touching the hoop.

NOTE

1. J. Sanborn, *Bag of Tricks: 180 Great Games* (Florissant, CO: Search Publications, 1984), 25.

Human Knot

Items Needed: At least some flexible family members

Directions: Have everyone stand in a circle and grab hands with two other family members. Make sure you are holding on to two different people. Now, without letting go, untangle yourselves until you are back in a circle.

So What? Just like when the family has a job to get done, it is important to learn to work together as a family. Someone unexpected may come up with the idea that makes everything work. It is important to learn to listen to and try everyone's solutions. This game is the perfect way to demonstrate this idea.

Wormhole

Items Needed: Rope, string, or a hula hoop

Directions: If using rope or string, tie it together so it is securely in a circle. With your whole family working together, you all have to figure out how to get everyone through the rope, or wormhole, in a different way. You can have someone jump through or do a handstand and have everyone pull it up. The only rule is that no one can go through the same way as someone else. Just watch as your family creativity shines.

So What? It is important to have an open mind and realize that no matter how small or different, everyone in the family can contribute and has good ideas. This game helps our families to think creatively and practice ways of solving problems together.

● ● ● ● ● ● ● **The Twisted Stand**

Items Needed: A family ready to work together (or at least ready to learn how)

Directions: Start this game out in partners, with every pair sitting back-to-back. Have everyone lock arms and then stand up by leaning against each other. When a pair has successfully done this, put them with another group and have them all lock arms and try to stand. Keep adding people to the group until the whole family is linked and is able to stand up without letting go.

So What? Family members need to learn to be there for each other when they need help. Sometimes in your life, you will come to things that you just can't do on your own. Family members need to realize that it is not only okay, it is a *great* idea to come to their family for help. This game will help your family members to remember they can always "lean" on each other.

● ● ● ● ● ● ● ● ● ● ● ● ●

Circle Sit

Items Needed: Room to move around

Directions: Have everyone stand in a circle, all facing the same way. Everyone should be looking at the back of the person in front of them. Get as tight as you can and then slowly sit down on the lap of the person behind you. This may take a few tries! Once you have mastered sitting down, walk in the circle by all moving the same foot at the same time. Sometimes it's helpful to have Dad yell, "Right! Left! Right!"

So What? Most kids want to stick out from the crowd and be different, in some way, from those around them. Unfortunately, going against the rules is sometimes a way of doing that. In this game, family members learn that they need to work together to accomplish things. If one person rushes to sit down, they fall. If one person steps with the wrong foot, they fall. If one person is not working with the family, it affects the whole unit. Kids need to know that their actions have consequences for the whole family and not just themselves. But if they all work together, they can do anything.

● ● ● ● ● ●   **World Record Ball Toss**

Items Needed: At least five items you can throw, such as soft balls, stuffed animals, and so forth.

Directions: Have everyone stand in a circle. One person starts out with a ball and throws it to another person that isn't standing next to them. Next, that person chooses a different person to throw to and so on until everyone has been thrown the ball. Remember who you threw the ball to because this will be the order you will be throwing in. Now, have the first person throw the ball to the person they selected in the previous round. After the ball has left their hands, start the second item around. See how many items you can get going at a time. Then see how long you can keep all of the items going.

So What? In order to make this game work, you need to work together and make sure you are communicating with each other. You may need to ensure eye contact is made before you throw, or you may choose to say the person's name you are throwing it to. No matter what changes you make, have your family work together to become faster or better in order to set the "world record." Then talk about how your family can use these communication skills and working together to solve daily problems like doing the laundry or dishes. When families work together, any activity can be fun and much more efficient!

● ● ● ● ● ● ● ● ● ● ● ● ● ●

Don't Spill the Beans

Items Needed: Plastics cups, and uncooked (hard) beans

Directions: Have family members hold a cup in their mouths without using their hands. They can do this by biting the rim with their teeth or clamping the cup with their lips. Get everyone in a line, and fill the first person's cup up with uncooked (hard) beans. Next, without using hands, the first person will pour all the beans into the next person's cup. The next person will pour the beans into the third person's cup, and the beans will be passed in this manner until they get to the very end. Can your family make it to the end without spilling the beans?

So What? Working together is very important in order to make families successful. If one person decided not to bend down lower or turn his head, the other person wouldn't be able to pour the beans in the next person's cup. In this same way, family members need to be flexible for each other. If no one will help each other, families will not get anything done. They need to be flexible and look for ways to make things easier for the other members of their family.

● ● ● ● ● ● ● ● ●   **Blind Tag**

Items Needed: Blindfolds, and a long rope

Directions: This game is best played outside around a large tree. Lay a rope around the tree with enough space for the members of your family to walk around in. Pair up with another person. One person in each partnership will be blindfolded. Lead all the blindfolded partners inside the circle, and pick one of them to be "it." When you say go, the game of tag is on! The trick is that the partners who can see have to tell their partner where to go to get away from the person that is "it." Once these members have played for a while, have the partners trade places. Now the people who could see before are now the ones playing blindfolded.

So What? Family members need to learn to trust each other and to pick each other out as the good voices in their lives. With all of the different people who are trying to tell your family what to do and who to be, it is important to learn to hear the voices of your family members, who are trying to lead you in the right direction.

● ● ● ● ● ● ● ● ● ● ● ● ●

• • • • • • • • • • • • •

Chapter 7

Improving Family Communication

• • • • • • • • • • • • •

Volcano Crossing

Items Needed: Paper plates

Directions: This game is best played outside. Here is your challenge: Your family has been stranded on a deserted island surrounded by hot lava. You need to get off the island before the volcano explodes again, but all you have are lava retardant paper plates. Somehow you must use the paper plates to get across the sea of lava without getting burned. If you do touch the lava, your paper plate will sink away and your family will have to share theirs with you in order for you to survive.

Have the group come up with a time they think they can accomplish this in. Give each person one paper plate, start the timer, and then tell them no one can talk! See how everyone works together. Take note of those who take the lead and those who follow. When you are finished, let everyone talk for a minute about how things went. Then make a plan, and set a new goal. Next, tell them they can talk, and see how much faster your family is able to get across the room.

Volcano Crossing

So What? Communication is key in family interactions. Families who have open communication are more likely to solve their problems at home in good ways instead of engaging in destructive behaviors. This game allows family members to experience how successful the family and each individual will be when they choose to communicate with others.

● ● ● ● ● ● ● ● ● ●   **Memory**

Items Needed: Paper, and pens

Directions: Start out in partners, sitting down with your backs against each other. Give the first partner a paper with a picture already drawn onto it. Without letting the second partner see the picture, blindfold him and give him a blank paper and a pen. Then, have the first partner give the second partner verbal instructions on how to draw the picture. Make sure the first partner explains where certain shapes are on the paper. When the partners think they are finished, take the blindfold off and have them look at each other's papers. The pictures will probably be very different. Next, do it again but have the first partner be the one with the blindfold and have the second one explain (with a different picture).

So What? Many times, the way family members think about something is not the way someone else in the family thinks about something. Even when they try to explain something to each other, family members may not fully understand what they mean. When family members have conflicts with people, they need to realize that everyone has different perspectives. They need to think about where other people are coming from and how they can better help others see their point of view.

● ● ● ● ● ● ● ● ● ● ● ● ● ●

Signs

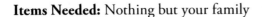

Items Needed: Nothing but your family

Directions: Have your family start out this game in a circle. Everyone in the circle needs to choose a sign that they want to be theirs. These signs can be anything that doesn't make noise, from tugging on your ear to pulling on your big toe. One person starts out in the middle and closes his eyes. Meanwhile, the group picks one person to start out with "the sign," which just means they are "it." The person in the middle opens his eyes and tries to figure out who has "the sign."

The person who has the sign needs to pass it to other people without getting caught. To pass a sign, do the sign of another person, like pulling on your ear. In order to actually give the sign to someone else, that person has to do his sign back to you in order to accept it. Once that person has accepted the sign, he must do someone else's sign to and pass it on without getting caught.

When the person in the middle suspects she has found the person with the sign, she asks, "Do you have the sign?" If the person does, he is now in the middle. If he doesn't have the sign, play resumes until someone is caught. Remember, if the person you are passing the sign to does not see you, or just doesn't do his sign back to you, you still have the sign!

So What? This is a great game to get your family thinking about communication. In the game, family members may want to pass a sign, but someone is not looking. Many times in life someone may really need to tell a family member something, but that person is just not paying attention, or is too busy. This game will help family members see the importance of paying attention to each other and using eye contact when communicating with one another. It can also help family members to start thinking about non-verbal communication and how it could be used to express different feelings and emotions in the family.

● ● ● ● ● ● ● ● **Think as I Think**

Items Needed: Blindfolds

Directions: In this game the family is divided into pairs. One person in each pair has a blindfold on and the other person cannot talk throughout the activity. The person who cannot talk is given tasks that he has to get his partner to do, such as moving a chair to the other side of the room, picking up legos and placing them back into their bucket, or folding up a blanket. Any tasks can be used in this game. When the partnership completes these tasks, have them trade places and give them a new list of tasks to complete.

So What? Learning different ways to communicate and express ourselves is an important trait to build as families. When family members feel like they have options in expressing their emotions, they are less likely to get angry and frustrated with each other. Taking away the basic ways of communication will push your family members to be creative and find new ways to express themselves to each other.

Variations: If you would like to up the challenge (and if you're up for a little messiness), have each partnership try and complete a recipe. The person who is blindfolded is the only one who can touch any of the items. The other partner has to remain silent.

● ● ● ● ● ● ● ● ● ● ● ● ●

Feelings before Facts • • • • • • •

Items Needed: Prep time, and paper

Directions: This game will need a little bit of preparation. First, you must type up a list of silly phrases like: "Your grandma wears army boots." Or "Somebody's stole me lucky charms." Print these out and cut them up into strips. Once you have this done, get your family together and brainstorm six different feelings that they feel on a regular basis such as happy, sad, flirtatious, angry, excited, and so forth. Number each of the feelings. For example, 1=happy, 2=sad, and so forth.

Put the silly phrases folded over in a bowl, and have one family member pick a phrase. Then, have him roll the die without letting anyone see the number. Next, have the family member say the phrase with the corresponding feeling with it. Guess the feeling he is displaying while saying the phrase. It can be quite hilarious. Try saying "Anybody want a peanut?" with a flirtatious feeling behind it. Your whole family will be rolling on the floor.

So What? Sometimes, family members don't always say things that they mean. If they make someone upset, it is important for them to realize it so they can fix it. When people talk to you, you need to listen to their feelings behind what they're saying. Even if mom and dad are upset, they probably are trying to help everyone to be better. If family members listen for the feelings behind the words, they will know that their parents love them and want to help them succeed.

• • • • • • • • • • • • • •

● ● ● ● ● ● ● **String Geometry**

Items Needed: String or yarn, and blindfolds

Directions: Tie the string to make a large circle. Make sure everyone is securely blindfolded. With everyone holding onto the string at all times with at least one hand, your family must create the necessary geometric shapes. When you think you have the shape, take your blindfolds off to see. If you have, move on to the next shape. If it is not quite the right shape, loosen up the string, put on your blindfolds, and try it again. Start out with easy shapes such as a circle, square, or triangle. Then move to polygons, two triangles touching on one corner, or a hematroblia. Okay, so that last one isn't really a shape, but see what fun shapes you can come up with.[1]

So What? Working together as a family and trying to communicate without being able to see is a challenge. No one quite knows how the shape looks, and everyone must take part in making sure the string in front of them is in the right place. In families everyone needs to make sure to do their part and communicate what is going on. If we never check in to make sure we are in line with our family's plan, we will end up with some pretty weird shapes!

NOTE

1. J. Sanborn, *Bag of Tricks: 180 Great Games*, 31.

● ● ● ● ● ● ● ● ● ● ● ● ●

How's Yours?

Items Needed: Lots of creative family members

Directions: Get everyone in a circle and have one person leave the room. As a group, pick something you are going to describe that everyone has, such as hair, shoes, bathroom, mothers (be careful with that one). Once you have decided, let the other person come back into the room. He or she must now go around the circle and ask members of the group, "How's yours?" Members in the circle answer that question giving a one or two word description of the selected subject. For example, if the item selected is "your hair," after being asked the question, answers might possibly be curly, brown, messy, and so forth. Based upon the answers she receives, the person in the middle tries to guess what everyone is describing.

So What? This hilarious game is perfect to help everyone realize the different perspectives and personalities in the family. Even though you are all describing the same thing, everyone describes it differently because we all think differently. When family members are angry with someone else in the family, we need to remember that they might not be thinking the same thing as others are. That makes it really important to talk to them, and try to look at the situation from their point of view.

Minefield

Items Needed: Lots of random objects, and blindfolds

Directions: To set up your minefield, you will need to fill a large space with many different objects, like water bottles or balled-up blankets. Everyone will need to cross the minefield without touching anything in it. The trick is, all players will be blindfolded when they cross. Have everyone first try to cross it without any help. Most likely no one will make it across without hitting something. Next, pair your family up, and let one person in each pair take his blindfold off. This person can now lead her partner to the other side by telling him where to step and what obstacles are in his way.

So What? Sometimes family members don't want to listen to the wise counsel of others, but instead want to figure things out for themselves. If they don't listen to family members, like their parents who can see what they can't and who may have been in the same situation before, they will have a very bumpy road. On the other hand, if they choose to let their family help, they will pass by many obstacles and eventually make it successfully to wherever or whatever they want to accomplish.

● ● ● ● ● ● ● ● ● ● ● ● ● ●

Chapter 8

Developing Family Unity:
One for All and All for One

● ● ● ● ● ● ● ● ● ● ● ● ● ●

Peas in a Pod

Items Needed: One large sheet or blanket, and lots of space

Directions: This game is best played in a big field, but you can make it work in the house if you make sure the pathway is clear. This is a race against yourselves. Wrap everyone in the blanket, bring the bottom edge up, and then time yourselves to see how fast you can make it across the field (or through the house) without anyone falling out of the blanket.

So What? This game teaches the family that no one gets left behind. Family members can't win the game without everyone staying in the blanket, just like your family couldn't be complete without everyone in it. Even though things may be hard, we need to work together to accomplish our goals and not let anyone fall out.

Rope Rebounding

Items Needed: A large rope

Directions: Firmly tie a rope into a large circle. Have everyone get inside of the circle. Next, have everyone lean back. Then have two people who are across from each other trade places. While they are trading places, everyone else leans back even more. Then, when the two get to their spots, they lean back on the rope and two other people bounce off and trade places. If everyone leans back just right, you can get a neat rhythm going. Make sure not to run into each other![1]

So What? Family members all have different places in their lives that they need to go: school, work, the store, and so forth. Sometimes it might feel like they are all going in opposite directions, but if families work together to make sure everyone is doing what they need to be doing, their family rhythm will be perfect!

NOTE

1. T. Orlick, *Cooperative Games and Sports: Joyful Activities for Everyone* (Champaign, IL: Human Kinetics, 2006).

● ● ● ● ● ● ● ● ● ●   **Bridges**

Items Needed: A soft place to fall

Directions: For this game, have everyone get into partners. Starting out with a partner your size will be easier. Have everyone put their hands against their partner's and hold their arms out straight. Hands must stay touching the entire time. As you lean against each other to keep from falling, keep taking baby steps back and see how far you can go. Mark how far back everyone went and see if you can increase your trust by leaning farther the next time. (Pillows in between the players may be helpful to soften falls.)

So What? You can always count on your family. Families are there to help each other, and family members need to make sure that they are someone that each member of the family can lean on for support. Remember: It won't be long till everyone will need someone to lean on!

● ● ● ● ● ● ● ● ● ● ● ● ● ●

Rolling Targets

● ● ● ● ● ● ● ●

Items Needed: Tennis balls, and a hula hoop

Directions: Split the family into two teams and have them stand in two lines, spread out about ten feet apart. Pick one person to be the roller. This person takes the hula hoop and rolls it down the lane of people. While the hula hoop is rolling by, everyone needs to try and throw their tennis ball through the hoop. Every ball that goes through the rolling hoop is a point for your team. Have each team alternate who the roller is until everyone has had a turn. Now, count up your points and the team with the most wins![1]

So What? Sometimes the goals or targets family members have in their lives are difficult to hit. They may not get it the first time, but with enough practice, they are bound to hit their goal. Even so, doing this alone would not be any fun. Families are there to encourage each other. What better way is there to go for a goal than when surrounded by family?

NOTE

1. A. Heaton, *Double Fun*, 25.

● ● ● ● ● ● ● ● ● ● ● ● ●

Do You Know Your Family?

Items Needed: Paper, and all the random facts about family members you can remember

Directions: Just like it is important for newlyweds to get to know each other, it is just as important for families to do the same thing! For this game have everyone come ready with all their facts about their family members. You can either have teams of two challenge each other, or have the whole family play against each other. Come up with questions that will test your family's knowledge of each other.

Example questions

1. If this family member could be any animal, what would he be?

2. If this family member has a fruit basket, what would she eat first: an apple, a banana, or an orange?

3. What is the color of this family member's toothbrush?

4. What is the one thing this family member is known for saying?

5. What does this family member want to be when they grow up?

6. If this family member could travel anywhere in the world, where would he go?

7. What is this family member's favorite movie?

8. What is this family member's biggest pet peeve?

9. What object could this family member not live without?

10. What piece of clothing do you see this family member in the most?

After asking a question, have everyone write down the answer for themselves. Then, write down what you think your partner or the other members of the family would say. If you correctly guess what other

Do You Know Your Family?

family members wrote down about themselves, you or your team get a point. The person who has the most points at the end, not only wins, but knows more about their family members than anyone else—yes!

So What? Part of being a family is knowing the little details about each other's lives. In most families, Mom is probably the master of this, but wouldn't it be great if we all knew the little details of each other? This is a humorous game to help you really get to know your family. That way, the next time you call your little sister a monkey, you'll know she really takes it as a compliment!

Tug-Tug-Tug-of-War

Items Needed: A rope

Directions: Tie your rope in a circle with a good knot that won't come out under a lot of pressure. Have two people start inside the circle, holding onto the rope on opposite sides. Create two goal lines that are on opposite sides. Assign a goal line to each team. On go, each person needs to run the toward his goal line. Each person tries to pull the other person across his goal line with them. The goal lines will be on opposite sides, so there will be lots of pulls and tugs. If you have a small family member, try adding on another family member to his side who can help pull. Soon you'll have the whole family in on this crazy tug![1]

So What? Just when you think you can't tug any more, your family steps in to save the day. Families are there to help each other when someone is in need. Even if it takes everybody, family members should support each other always and know that their family won't stop until they've reached their goal.

NOTE

1. A. Heaton, *Double Fun*, 35.

Family Circle

Items Needed: A rope, and lots of room

Directions: Using a rope that is tied in a circle, have everyone spread themselves out evenly on all sides of the rope. (Be sure to remove any sharp objects in case someone falls!) Holding onto the rope, have everyone lean back at the same time. See how your weight helps to keep everyone up. One at a time, call off a member of the family to let go of the rope. You will have to readjust to keep from falling every time.[1]

So What? Family members all need to pull equal weight in their family. When one person decides to break the rules or is rude to another family member, the whole family has to readjust or risk falling. Families must realize that they all hold each other up. They are counting on each member to help in keeping the family in balance.

Variations: Just for fun, try to make a wave while everyone is holding onto the rope. See if you can get two waves going at the same time. What happens if you have two waves working in opposite directions? *Crash!*

NOTE

1. The Walter Family

Two Heads Are Better than One

Items Needed: Balloons

Directions: For this game you will need one balloon for every two people in your family. Set up an obstacle course that includes things like climbing up stairs, going down a slide, running, hopping over a rope, and so forth. First, have all family members individually do the obstacle course while keeping the balloon on their head (without using their hands). Most likely, you will find that everyone will not be able to do it alone. Next, have everyone get into partners and hold one balloon between their heads. See how fast each partnership can make it through the obstacle course without dropping the balloon. When they drop it, have them come back and encourage them to come up with a strategy that will help them on their next try.

So What? This cooperative game will help each member of the family learn to work with one another. They were not able to keep the balloon up by themselves, but with help, the course wasn't so hard. Sometimes a family member may need help figuring out their homework or knowing how to deal with a problem at school. Family members should always feel like they can come to their family for help with their problems. Remember: two heads are better than one!

Buck Buck   ● ● ● ● ● ● ● ● ●

Items Needed: Lots of space, and room for running

Directions: This game can be a lot fun, but you have to make sure you are super careful and that you plan strategically. It is best played on a grassy field or anywhere else where there will be a soft landing. Have two to four people (depending on the size of your group) hunch over and hold onto each other's backs, creating a kind of flat platform so other people will be able to be stable when they are on top of the "mound." Once they are secure, send one person to take a running start toward the group while yelling, "Buck Buck One!" and jump onto the backs of the bottom players. Then, have the next person do the same yelling, "Buck Buck Two!" See how many people you can get stacked up on the "mound" until the people forming the platform on the bottom fall or someone slides off the top!

So What? This game is perfect to help develop unity in the family. Your family can be a firm foundation for you to always trust. Families will hold each other up no matter what. If they fall, they all fall together.

WARNING: This game can be very dangerous. Please use caution as bodies are being flailed. The author and publisher are *not* responsible for any broken Buck Bucks!

● ● ● ● ● ● ● ● ● ● ● ● ●

● ● ● ● ● ●   **Amazing Advertisers**

Items Needed: Large paper, and art supplies (paint, markers, crayons, and so forth)

Directions: Give a large piece of paper to each person in the family. Put the names of everyone in your family on a piece of paper. Have each family member draw a name out of a hat. Next, everyone needs to create a billboard sign for the person who's name they drew. The billboard is an advertisement to the world about why they would want to be this family member's friend. Draw pictures of the family member, positive attributes that she has, or anything that would help others to see what a great person she is. In the end, other family members can add onto the billboards.

So What? It is so important to lift each other up as a family. Complimenting family members and supporting them in their strengths will help increase their confidence and ability to handle tough situations. Imagine the strength of your family if you were always working to build each other up!

● ● ● ● ● ● ● ● ● ● ● ● ● ●

Spiderweb

Items Needed: A big ball of yarn

Directions: Have everyone sit in a circle and pick one person to start out with the yarn. Have the first person choose someone to throw it to. Before throwing it, the first person needs to say something he admires about that person. Then have the first person throw the ball while still holding onto the string. After it goes across the circle a few times, you have made a spider's web.

So What? Using the spider web as a visual, this game has a powerful effect on how your family is connected to each other through the love that you have. Family members all admire different things about each other, and when they pull together, they make something beautiful. Helping family members express their feelings for each other will help make your home a happier place!

● ● ● ● ● ● ● ●   **Guard the Chair**

Items Needed: A large space, and a chair

Directions: Have your family create a large circle around a chair, and pick one person to be the guard. Everyone in the outside circle wants to try and touch the chair without getting tagged. If you get tagged, you must go back to the outside circle. If you are tagged three times, you are out and you have to wait for another round. Whoever touches the chair gets to be the next guard.[1]

So What? This game helps you to learn to stand up and guard your family. Family members should stand up for each other if anyone is making fun of them, and they definitely shouldn't be the ones making fun of each other. They will all feel safer at school, at home, and in all places, knowing that they have a family who is always looking out for them.

NOTE

1. F. W. Harris, *Games* (Harris, 1962), 39.

● ● ● ● ● ● ● ● ● ● ● ● ●

Dragon Tails

Items Needed: Lots of space

Directions: A field or another large space would be perfect for this crazy game. Have your family get into one long line with everyone holding onto each other by the shoulders or waist. The object of the game is for the front person to catch the person in the very back of the line. Everyone must move strategically to avoid the capture of the back person since everyone is connected. If the person in the back is caught, the front person goes to the back of the line and now it's their turn to be chased!

So What? In a family, only looking out for yourself doesn't cut it. Families need to make sure that they are looking out for all members. Everyone will take a turn at the back of line where they need help. It is up to the family to support and guide that person out of trouble.

● ● ● ● ● ● ● ●   **Lean on Me**

Items Needed: Space to run (or hop)

Directions: This is a basic game of tag except there is one twist: you can only use one foot. You also can't lean on anything to support you except another family member. The person who is "it" is also required to stand on one foot. If they put their foot down, they have to stay in that spot for ten seconds (while everyone runs away). For the rest of the players, putting your foot down means you are now "it!"

So What? Your family should be one of your greatest support systems. Helping children realize this is often a struggle, but with games like this one, your family will unite and realize that they can always come to a family member if they are in need of help.

● ● ● ● ● ● ● ● ● ● ● ● ●

Slap in Time

Items Needed: Concentration

Directions: Lay on your stomachs in a big circle on the floor, with your faces toward each other. Put your hands on the ground with your arms interlocked so that your hands are not right next to each other.

The point of the game is to try and keep the pattern going around the circle. The pattern starts clockwise with someone slapping their hand once. Then the hand next to them slaps once. It goes on like this until someone slaps twice. When this is done, the direction of the slaps change. If anyone slaps out of order, he has to take out his hand. The person with a hand left at the end of the game wins.

So What? Members in the family have their turn to do different things. They can't all learn to drive at once. Sometimes it may be hard to wait your turn or to see others getting things that you want. Family members just have to learn the order of their family and do their part when it comes time for them to perform.

• • • • • • • • • • • • • •

Chapter 9

Good Lessons to Learn

• • • • • • • • • • • • • •

Fortunately, Unfortunately

Items Needed: Paper, and pens

Directions: In this game, everyone sits in a circle. One person writes down something unfortunate that has happened to her recently. Then, she passes the paper to the person next to her and that person then writes how that unfortunate event has a fortunate spin to it. Continue this pattern until everyone has had a chance to write.

Examples:

Unfortunately . . . I will be getting my wisdom teeth out next week

Fortunately . . . Brushing my teeth won't take so long every day!

So What? This game helps family members to develop different perspectives on the things that happen to them. Sometimes family members may find themselves in difficult situations, but if they can learn to help each other look on the bright side, they will find it much easier to get through their own difficulties.

Fortunately, Unfortunately

Variations: You can play this game making one long story. One person starts the story and then the next person continues it with fortunately, the next person with unfortunately, and so on.

Box Ball

Items Needed: A large rope, and a ball

Directions: Tie your rope in a circle. Have everyone get inside of the circle, leaning back against the rope. Start kicking the ball around and see how many times you can kick it to each other without the ball going out of the rope. Now try moving, walking in the same direction, while kicking the ball—tricky![1]

So What? Most of the time in your life, you will have different rules or boundaries that you have to live by. Sometimes those rules might seem restricting, but with the help of your family, they can become fun or easier to handle. Instead of focusing on what you can't do, like moving out of the circle, let's focus on what you can, like kicking the ball.

Note

1. T. Orlick, *Cooperative Games and Sports: Joyful Activities for Everyone.*

"Feet"ing Frenzy

Items Needed: A balloon

Directions: Have everyone lay down on their backs close together. Throw one balloon in the air. Your family needs to work together to see how many times the balloon can hit a different person's feet without touching the ground. Make sure everyone gets a chance to keep it up. After a few attempts, have your family stop and reposition themselves where they think will be the best way in order to keep the balloon up. (Maybe put littler kids in the middle and bigger kids on the outside, or have a set person that each family member passes the balloon to.) Now see how many times you can hit it. I bet it will be faster.

So What? Sometimes you need to stop and change what you are doing in order to make it more successful. It's okay to try new ideas and if they don't work, stop and try a different idea. "If at first you don't succeed . . . try, try again!"

Variations: You can also do this activity standing up in a circle or with different objects like stuffed animals or a beach ball. Throw a twist into the game—have everyone only use their left hand or even their heads. You'll be world champions in no time!

The Family Band

Items Needed: Household objects, and old paper goods

Directions: Give everyone in your family fifteen minutes to go around the house to find a "musical instrument." These instruments could be made by blowing in half-filled bottles, banging on old milk jugs, scratching sand paper together, or anything else you can come up with. When everyone has found an instrument, get together and come up with a rhythm that includes the sounds of everyone. Maybe you could even come up with your own song and start a family band!

So What? All family members have different sounds (talents) that they bring to the family. One child may be really smart, while another is great at crafts. Everyone is important and all the talents together make up your family. If someone were missing, it just wouldn't sound right.

Variations: Play some of your family's favorite songs. Play the song on the stereo and have everyone try to follow along with their instrument. Then, turn the stereo off and see what you can do with just your family. You may be surprised at how similar you sound (or you may fall on the floor laughing).

One-word Story

Items Needed: Creative family members

Directions: With your family all in a circle, go around and tell a story one word at a time. Start with one person saying a word and then have each person around the circle add one word at a time until you have one crazy tale!

So What? Your kids may not like writing stories for school, but sometimes when you work together, things you never liked doing could be a blast. Next, lets try doing chores!

Variations: If it's too easy for your family, have them do this without using *and* or *but*. It's a lot more difficult than it sounds!

● ● ● ● ● ● ● ● **In Your Shoes**

Items Needed: Shoes from every family member

Directions: Have everyone in your family bring out their wildest pair of shoes. Put all of the shoes in a pile. Next, have everyone close their eyes and grab the pair that is closest to them. Put on the pair of shoes you picked and figure out who's they are. You will now be that person. Get half of the family to get up first and give them a scenario like a day at Disneyland, at the grocery store, or ordering food at a restaurant. Next, have that half of the family act out the scenario as the person whose shoes they are wearing.

So What? Sometimes it is hard to see life from another person's perspective and because of this, it can be hard to get along when you both think or do things differently. This game gives everyone the opportunity to think about life from the perspective of another family member. Children will be reminded that it's fun to be different and that they need to accept and love each other for their differences.

● ● ● ● ● ● ● ● ● ● ● ● ●

Who's the Leader

Items Needed: One clever family

Directions: Everyone stands in a circle and one person is chosen to go out of the room. While they are out, a person in the circle is chosen to be the leader. Bring the person back and have them stand in the middle of the circle. The leader does an action that everyone else in the circle must copy. The leader changes their action after doing it a few times, and the person in the middle tries to guess who the leader is. Actions can be anything from sitting on your hands to jumping up and down. Don't make any noises though, just movements. When the person in the middle guesses who the leader is, the leader is now in the middle and a new leader is chosen.[1]

So What? People can tell who your leader is by your actions. The saying "Actions speak louder than words" is very true. The way families act can tell others a lot about the people that they are.

NOTE

1. The Walter Family

Game Index

About the Author

BRITTANY LAREE THOMPSON WAS BORN and raised in Southern California by parents who definitely knew how to have fun. When she would come home from school growing up, her mom would have an activity just waiting for the children. They never had time to be bored because of the games that needed to be played. Brittany credits her mom for her love of recreation! Brittany has received a Bachelor's Degree from Brigham Young University in Recreational Management and Youth Leadership, with an emphasis in Therapeutic Recreation. She is a Certified Therapeutic Recreation Specialist and loves changing the lives of those she works with through recreation. She loves camping, biking, hiking, snowboarding, cooking when it doesn't burn, dancing when no one's watching, singing in the car, and, of course, playing games with her wonderful husband and family.

0 26575 52224 2